The Musician's Joke Book

The Musician's Joke Book

◆◆◆◆◆◆◆◆

Knowing the Score

N.J. Groce

Schirmer Books
An Imprint of Simon & Schuster Macmillan
New York

Prentice Hall International
London Mexico City New Delhi Singapore Sydney Toronto

Schirmer Books
An Imprint of Simon & Schuster Macmillan
1633 Broadway
New York, New York 10019

Library of Congress Catalog Card Number: 93-42310

Printed in the United States of America

Printing Number

 2 3 4 5 6 7 8 9 10

Design: Rob Carangelo

Groce, N. J.
    The musician's joke book: knowing the score/ N. J. Groce.
        p.   cm.
    ISBN 0-02-864680-0 (alk. paper)
    1. Music—Humor.   I. Title.
    ML65.G76   1996
    780' .207—dc20   95-42310
                                                          CIP
                                                          MN

This paper meets the requirements of ANSI/NISO Z39.28-1992
(Permanence of Paper).

INTRODUCTION

A LARGE PART OF A MUSICIAN'S LIFE involves waiting: waiting for the stage to be set up, waiting for the rest of the ensemble to unpack and warm up, waiting to finish tuning, waiting for the score to be passed out, waiting for the sound check to be completed, waiting for the concert to begin, waiting for intermission to end, and waiting for the van, bus, train, or plane to take you to the next concert. Perhaps because of this, musicians often tell jokes to pass the time. During the past few years, a "cycle" or "fad" of musician jokes has emerged. Some of these jokes are adaptations of generic stupid-people jokes, what folklorists refer to as "noodle" or "numskull" jokes. Others, specific to musicians and knowledgeable music lovers, presume that the listeners share a common base of specialized knowledge about music and the experiences of musicians.

As in other joke cycles, certain subsets are singled out for more derision than others. For example, among orchestral musicians, violists are identified with what, for want of a better term, I call the "bottom-of-the-feeding-chain." Jokes about musical incompetence or moronic behavior are often told as viola jokes. Competing for lowest-of-the-low honors in other musical genres are drummers in rock; accordion players in popular, folk, and traditional music; and banjoists in bluegrass and Country & Western. Why? Who knows? In the case of violas, there is a widespread assumption among classical musicians that viola parts are much less demanding than those written for violin. Then, too, music teachers often urge less-gifted violin students to take up the viola. The accordion might have been singled out because of its

long association with wedding receptions, ethnic ensembles, and too many renditions of "Lady of Spain." I suspect banjos were initially "picked on" because of their association with "hillbillies," "rustics," and "hicks." And drummers? Drums are not always the most subtle of instruments, and a bad drummer is in an unparalleled position to wreak havoc on even the largest musical ensemble. All this is speculation; however, a disproportionately large number of musician jokes do involve violists, banjoists, drummers, and accordion players.

Although some of the jokes in this book date back at least to the 1960s and '70s, most of them were collected during the last ten years from classical, rock, folk, and jazz musicians in and around New York City. Not all musicians tell these jokes, but most professional musicians will have heard at least some of them. I have found that musicians are frequently somewhat reluctant to tell jokes about their own instrument. Such loyalty is commendable. However, the same narrators have no qualms about switching the focus of their latest joke to the instruments played by their current listeners; this might be a coincidence, but I doubt it. Jokes are usually circulated through oral transmission, but sometimes also appear in union newspapers, trade journals, or professional magazines. An interesting recent development has been the appearance of some of these jokes on the "information superhighway," the internet. It is reassuring to know that virtual reality can be really funny, and that poor taste is in no danger of becoming passé.

The author wishes to thank all the friends and colleagues who have assisted with this project. Although most would probably prefer to remain anonymous, I would nonetheless like to thank Ray Allen, Paula Ballan, Trudy Callahan, John C. Casey, Erik Frandsen, Barbara Haws, Catherine Jacobs, Tracy Strann Landsman, Laurence Libin, Michael Licht, Danny Litwin, Ric Luftglass, John McCusker, Don Meade, Anina Karmen-Meade, William Monical, Fred Oster, Jerry O'Sullivan, Daniel Peck, Carl Rahkonen, Darrell Reich, Alan Reid, John Reynolds, Alistair Russell, Henry Sapoznik, Debra Siegel, Robert Sheldon, Anne Underwood, and Andy Wallace. Finally, special thanks to Heather Wood, who was "instrumental" in bringing this project to fruition.

xi

Conductors and Composers

IT'S ALWAYS POSSIBLE TO ARGUE about who has more status in the musical world, but many musicians, critics, and music lovers think in terms of a hierarchy that begins with conductors, composers, and orchestral string players. I don't buy into this system of rankings myself, but we might as well begin by making fun of the "top-of-the-feeding-chain."

◆ What's the difference between a conductor and a sack of fertilizer? The sack.

◆ Why are conductors' hearts coveted for transplants? They've had little use.

◆ A musician called the orchestra's office and asked for the conductor. He was told that the conductor had died. He then called back twenty-five more times, and each time the receptionist gave him the same message. Finally, she asked why he kept calling. "I just like to hear you say it," he replied.

◆ Many conductors are revered for their gentle, astute, and judicious guidance; most aren't. When Eugene Ormandy led the Philadelphia Symphony Orchestra, the musicians recorded the following bon mots:

"Who is sitting in that empty chair?"

"I guess you thought I was conducting, but I wasn't."

"Start three bars before something."

"The tempo remains pp."

"Bizet was a very young man when he composed this symphony, so play it soft."

"I don't mean to make you nervous, but unfortunately I have to."

"This is a very democratic organization, so let's take a vote. All those who disagree with me, raise their hands."

"Why do you always insist on playing when I'm trying to conduct?"

◆ Knock, knock. Who's there? Philip Glass.

Knock, knock. Who's there? Philip Glass.

Knock, knock. Who's there? Philip Glass.

Knock, knock. Who's there? Philip Glass . . .

◆ <u>Music</u>: A complex organization of sounds, akin to noise and cacophony, that is set down by the composer and incorrectly interpreted by the conductor, who is disregarded by the musicians, the result of which is ignored by the audience.

- ◆ Famous piano quote: "A piano is a piano is a piano." *Gertrude Steinway*

- ◆ What's the difference between an orchestra and a bull? On a bull, you have the horns up front and the asshole in the back, while in the orchestra . . .

- ◆ Orchestra Personnel Standards:
  (N.B. The author has encountered numerous versions of the following list. This one was passed along by a French horn player, obviously.

Conductor

Leaps tall buildings in a single bound.

Is more powerful than a locomotive.

Is faster than a speeding bullet.

Walks on water.

Gives policy to God.

Concertmaster

Leaps short buildings in a single bound.

Is more powerful than a switch engine.

Is just as fast as a speeding bullet.

Walks on water if sea is calm.

Talks with God.

Oboe

Leaps short buildings with a running start and favorable winds.

Is almost as powerful as a switch engine.

Is almost as fast as a speeding bullet.

Walks on water in an indoor swimming pool.

Talks with God if special request is approved.

Trumpet

Barely clears a quonset hut.

Loses tug-of-war with locomotive.

Can fire a speeding bullet.

Swims well.

Is occasionally addressed by God.

Bassoon

Makes marks high on wall when trying to clear short buildings.

Is run over by locomotive.

Can sometimes handle a gun without inflicting self-injury.

Dog-paddles.

Talks to animals.

Second Violin

Runs into buildings.

Recognizes locomotives two times out of three.

Is not issued ammunition.

Can stay afloat with a life jacket.

Talks to walls, argues with self.

Manager

Falls over doorstep when trying to enter buildings.

Says "Look at the choo-choo."

Wets self with water pistol.

Plays in mud puddles.

Loses argument with self.

French Horn

Lifts buildings and walks under them.

Kicks locomotives off the tracks.

Catches speeding bullets with teeth and eats them.

Freezes water with a single glance.

Is God.

♦ What's the ideal weight of a conductor? 28 ounces, including the urn.

♦ Did you hear that Wurlitzer is going to merge with Xerox? They plan to sell reproductive organs.

♦ The conductor of a provincial orchestra was having a terrible day. They were scheduled to play Beethoven's Ninth on a sweltering summer's evening, but the chorus from the local college didn't arrive for rehearsal until 6:00! As they were finally taking their seats, the air conditioning system broke down, and the stage-hands had to bring in some giant fans. The fans, in turn, created such a draft that the conductor had to tie the score to his stand to keep it from blowing away. Then, sometime between 7:00 and 7:30, when he was frantically trying to rehearse the chorus, two cellists and all the bassists slipped out to the bar across the street, where they proceeded to partake of too much liquid refreshment. The cellists never returned at all, and the bass section came back dead drunk, just in time for the 8:00 curtain. Things didn't look promising, but the symphony went smoothly enough until the beginning of the last movement when, without warning, the air conditioning system failed again and the stagehands were obliged to turn on the fans full blast! At this point, the conductor gave up. What else could he do? There he was at the bottom of the Ninth, the score was tied, two men were out, the basses were loaded, and the fans were going wild!

♦ A jazz trumpeter was hired as a last-minute substitute for a symphony orchestra concert. He was doing a fine job of sight-reading his part until the slow movement when, after a long, subdued cello solo, he suddenly stood up and wailed out a spectacular, if unexpected, solo. The conductor was astonished, but the impromptu solo was so beautiful he didn't try to stop it. However, after the concert he rushed up to the jazz trumpeter and said: "I don't mean to criticize, that was truly one of the most beautiful and inspired musical experiences I've had for years, but what on earth made you do it?" "Well," the guy says, "my chart said 'Tac it,' so I did."

STRING INSTRUMENTS

CALLED "CHORDOPHONES" BY MUSICOLOGISTS, bowed string instruments such as violins, violas, violoncellos (usually called cellos for short), and double basses have a long and distinguished history, but you'd hardly know it from these jokes.

◆ How can you tell if a violin is out of tune? The bow is moving.

◆ Why do most people take an instant dislike to violinists? It saves time.

◆ Why are orchestra intermissions limited to 20 minutes? So they don't have to retrain the cellists.

◆ Why are violins smaller than violas? They're actually the same size, it's the violinists' heads that are larger.

◆ What's the difference between a cello and a coffin? The coffin has a dead person on the inside.

◆ How do you get a cello to sound beautiful? Sell it and buy a violin.

- How do you get a cellist to play *fortissimo*? Write "*pp, expressivo*" on the music.

- The conductor broke up a fight between the second violinist and the first oboist. "What's going on here?" he yelled. "This jerk just reached over and broke my reed," replied the oboist. "He had it coming," spat back the violinist. "He turned down one of my pegs, and now he won't tell me which one!"

- How many bass players does it take to change a light bulb? I, V, I, V . . .

- The publisher is doing really well with its violin book *A Tune a Day*. So well, in fact, that they're planning to publish an edition for violists entitled *A Tune a Week*. If that sells, they'll release *A Tune a Month* for cellists. And if that's a success, they're going to put out one just for double bass players entitled *Tune*.

- What do you call one pretty good violinist, one bad violinist, one failed violinist, and someone who hates violinists together in the same room? A string quartet.

- What do most violinists use for birth control? Their personalities.

◆ How can you tell the last chair violinist? He's the only one without a knife in his back.

◆ Why are violists' fingers like lightning? They rarely strike the same spot twice.

◆ Why is a viola like a Scud missile? Both are inaccurate and highly offensive.

◆ At a viola convention, the rumor went around that one of the participants could play hemidemisemiquavers (32d notes). A crowd of violists clustered around their gifted colleague and asked him if it was true. He said it was, so they asked him to prove it and play one.

- What do you call 500 violists buried up to their necks in sand? A good start. (Or insufficient sand!)

- Why are viola jokes so short? So violinists can remember them.

- What is the difference between a viola and a trampoline? You take your shoes off to jump on the trampoline.

- What's the difference between a viola and a vacuum cleaner? The vacuum has a better tone.

- How is a viola different from a lawn mower? You can tune a lawn mower.

- What's another difference between a viola and a lawn mower? The lawn mower vibrates.

- Why isn't a viola like a lawn mower? Nobody minds if you borrow their viola.

- Did you hear about the instant viola repair kit? [Hold up a match.]

- How is a viola like a jury trial? Everyone breathes a sigh of relief when the case is closed.

- What happens when a violist dies? They move him back one stand.

- How can you tell if there is a whole herd of violists outside your door? Nobody knows when to come in.

- What's the definition of the ultimate optimist? A violist with a beeper.

- What was the violist's first question after he finally got a professional position? "Would you like fries with that, sir?"

- How do you keep your violin from getting stolen? Put it in a viola case.

- What's the difference between a violist and a dog? A dog knows when to stop scratching.

- There's a room with Muammar Qaddafi, Saddam Hussein, and a viola player in it. You have a gun with only two bullets. What do you do? Use both bullets to kill the viola player, just to be sure.

- What's the best recording of Bartók's Viola Concerto? *Music Minus One.*

- What's unique about viola concertos? They're the only concertos in which the soloist plays the harmony.

- What is the world's best viola joke? Berlioz's "Harold in Italy."

- What's the difference between a viola and a cello? A cello burns longer.

- What's another difference between a viola and a cello? You can fit more violas into a trash compactor.

- What's the most challenging requirement for finalists in the International Viola Competition? A finalist must be able to hold his viola from memory.

- How do you get a violist to do a tremolo? Put a fermata over a whole note and mark it solo.

- Why is a violist like a terrorist? They both screw up Boeings.

- The last chair violist of the Minot, North Dakota, Symphony found a magic lamp,

22

and after rubbing it, a genie appeared and granted him three wishes. His first wish was to be an 80 percent better player than he was now. The genie granted him his wish and—poof!—he became the principal violist of the Minot, North Dakota, Symphony! Soon he was no longer satisfied with this, so he made his second wish—again to become an 80 percent better player than he was and—poof!—he became the principal violist in the Philadelphia Orchestra! Well, he still had one wish to go, and so after a few months in Philadelphia, he asked once more to become an 80 percent better player than he had been. Poof!—he was again promoted, this time to become the last chair violinist in the second violin section of the Minot, North Dakota, Symphony.

◆ What's the difference between the first stand of violas and the third stand of violas? About a measure and a half.

◆ Why don't viola players practice? The spirit is willing, but the Flesch is too hard.

◆ How many positions does a violist use? First, third, and emergency.

◆ Frustrated after several hours of rehearsing, the conductor turned to the orchestra and said, "Okay, let's start at bar 5." The principal violist thought for a minute and then raised his hand. "I'm sorry," he said, "but we don't have bar numbers."

◆ A violist was hiking in the mountains, and he came upon a shepherd tending a large flock of sheep. The violist took a fancy to the sheep, and asked the shepherd: "If I can guess how many sheep you have, can I have one?" The shepherd thought this was an odd request, but since he thought there was little chance that the violist could guess correctly, he said, "Sure." "You have 287," the violist correctly guessed, to the shepherd's utter astonishment. The excited violist then asked, "Can I pick out my sheep now?" and the shepherd grudgingly gave his permission.

    The violist selected his animal, picked it up, and swung it over his shoulders to carry it home. Just then, the shepherd had an idea: "If I guess your occupation, can I have my sheep back?" The violist was a bit surprised, but figured that it was unlikely that the shepherd would be able to guess what he did, so he agreed. "You're a violist, aren't you?" said the shepherd. "Amazing!" said the violist.

"But how did you know?" "Well," the shepherd responded, "put the dog down and we'll talk about it."

♦ What's the definition of atonal music? A violist playing Bach.

♦ What's the useless woody material around the F holes? A viola.

♦ There was a man who went to his doctor and was diagnosed with a terminal illness. He was very upset and asked the doctor if there was anything he could do to prolong his life. "Not really," said the doctor, "but perhaps you could do one thing . . . You could marry a viola player and move to Cleveland." "Will that make me live longer?" the man asked in disbelief. "No, not really," replied the doctor. "But it will sure seem that way."

♦ Why do violas make perfect murder weapons? They're the classic blunt instrument, and they never have any fingerprints on them.

♦ How do you make a violin sound like a viola? Sit in the back and don't play.

◆ Entry Exam for the BBC Symphony Orchestra's Viola section. (N.B.: The pass mark is 10 points. Be careful: score over 25 points and you'll be disqualified.)

1. Who wrote the following:

   a. Beethoven's Symphony No. 6

   b. Fauré's Requiem

   c. Wagner's Ring Cycle (5 points)

2. Tchaikovsky wrote six symphonies including Symphony No. 4. Name the other five. (5 points)

3. Explain "counterpoint" or write your name on the back of this paper. (10 points)

4. Can you explain "sonata form"? (Answer yes or no.) (5 points)

27

5. Domenico Scarlatti wrote 555 harpsichord sonatas for which instrument? (5 points)

6. Where would you normally expect to find the conductor during the performance? (15 points)

7. Arrange the following words into the name of a well-known Puccini opera: Bohème, La. (5 points)

8. Tosca is a character found in which Puccini opera? (10 points)

29

Woodwind and Brass Instruments

WOODWIND AND BRASS PLAYERS ARE NOTORIOUS joke tellers. Perhaps there are just too many wind players adept at producing hot air, or perhaps they spend too much time counting rests. The sixteenth-century goldsmith Benvenuto Cellini—according to Hector Berlioz—denounced a colleague by calling him "Scoundrel! Mounteback! Clown! Pedant! Eunuch! Flute-player!" The sentiment still seems to be widespread, as the following examples demonstrate.

- Famous woodwind quote: "There's nothing I like better than the sound of an oboe—unless it's the sound of a chicken caught in a vacuum cleaner."

- What's the difference between a sax and a chain saw? Vibrato.

- Two flutists are talking and one says to the other, "Who was that piccolo I saw you with last night?" "That was no piccolo, that was my fife."

- Famous oboe quote: "An ill wind that nobody blows good."

- A trombone player and a conductor are crossing the street. You are driving and cannot avoid them both. Which do you hit? The trombone player: business before pleasure.

◆ Why was the clarinetist staring at the orange juice bottle? Because the label said "Concentrate."

◆ What's the definition of a real nerd? Someone who owns his own alto clarinet.

◆ What do you call a bass clarinetist with half a brain? Gifted.

◆ A reminder: The English horn, which is neither English nor a horn, should not be confused with the French horn, which is German.

35

- Did you hear about the latest urban crime wave? Drive-by tuba solos.

- How many alto sax players does it take to change a light bulb? Five: one to handle the bulb, and four to contemplate how Charlie Parker would have done it.

- What's the difference between a good French horn player and Bigfoot? There have been sightings of Bigfoot.

- What's the range of a tuba? About 20 feet, if you have a good arm.

- How do you spot a trombonist's kids on a playground? They're they ones who don't know how to use the slide and can't swing.

- How does a trombonist answer the phone at a gig? "Hello, Domino's."

- What's the difference between the dead frog in the middle of the road and a dead trombonist? The skid marks in front of the frog.

- What's another difference between the dead frog and the dead trombonist? The frog was probably on his way to a gig.

- How do you make a trombone sound like a French horn? Put your hand up the bell and make a lot of mistakes.

- If you drop a viola and a tuba from the top floor of a tall building, which one hits the ground first? Who cares?

- What kind of calendar does a trombonist use for his gigs? "Career-at-a-Glance."

- What's the difference between a trombone and a chain saw? The chain saw sounds better in small ensembles.

- What's a tuba for? Oh, usually about 1 1/2" X 3 1/2" . . .

SINGERS

INSTRUMENTAL MUSICIANS TEND TO THINK of themselves as a different species than singers, who are, well, singers. Differences in training, repertoire, and—at least according to the instrumentalists—temperament help explain this deep division.

- What's the difference between a soprano and a terrorist? You can reason with the terrorist.

- What's another difference? Terrorists have sympathizers.

- If you throw a violist and a soprano off a cliff, which one would hit the ground first? The violist. The soprano would have to stop halfway down to ask directions.

- How many female singers does it take to sing "Crazy"? All of them.

- How do you know if there's a lead singer outside your door? You don't: She can't find the key and doesn't know when to come in.

- What's the difference between a soprano and a Porsche? Most musicians have never been in a Porsche.

- How many altos does is take to screw in a light bulb? None, they can't get up that high.

- What's the definition of an optimist? A choral director with a mortgage.

- Did you hear about the choral conductor who refused to program the *Messiah*? He felt he couldn't Handel it.

- Where is a tenor's resonance? Where his brain should be.

- How many tenors does it take to screw in a light bulb? Just one; he simply holds it up and the world revolves around him.

◆ What's the definition of a male quartet? Three men and a tenor.

◆ If you took all the tenors in the world and laid them end to end . . . it would be a good idea.

Definitions of Musical Terms

YOU MIGHT WANT TO FAMILIARIZE yourself with the following slightly skewed musical definitions. I've arranged them in alphabetical order, just in case you need to refer to them quickly in a musical emergency.

Accent: an unusual manner of pronunciation

Accidentals: wrong notes

Ad libitum: a premiere

Agitato: one's state of mind when a finger slips in the middle of a solo

Agnus Dei: a woman composer best known for her church music

Altered chord: a sonority that has been spayed

Attaca: "Fire at will!"

Augmented fifth: a 36-ounce bottle

Bar line: a gathering of thirsty people, which often contains one or more musicians

Bravo: a spontaneous expression of appreciation on the part of the audience following a particularly trying performance

Breve: the way a sustained note sounds when you run out of air

Cadence: when everybody hopes you're going to stop, but you don't
    Final cadence: when they *force* you to stop

Cantus firmus: the part you get to play when you can only play four notes

Chords: a particular type of pants, for example, "He wears chords"

Chromatic scale: an instrument for weighing that indicates half pounds

Clef: something to jump off if you have to teach high school music

Coloratura soprano: a singer who has great trouble finding the proper note, but who has a wild time hunting for it

Conduct: types of air vents in a prison, especially designed to prevent escapes

Conductor: a musician who's adept at following many people at the same time

49

Counterpoint: a favorite device of many Baroque composers, all of whom are dead, though no direct connection between these two facts has been established; still taught in many conservatories as a form of punishment

Countertenor: a singing waiter

Crescendo: a reminder to the performer that he has been playing too loudly

Cut time: when you're going twice as fast as everybody else

Da capo al fine: "I like your hat!"

Detache: indicates that the trombonists are to play with their slides removed

Discord: used in contradistinction to Datcord

Ductia: (Latin, second declension) a lot of mallards

Dominant chord: something used to tie up groupies

Espressivo: close eyes and play with a wide vibrato; a type of Italian coffee

Estampie: what you put on letters in Quebec

Fermata: a brand of girdle made especially for opera singers

Fine: "That sounded just great!"

Flat: what happens to a tonic if you forget to screw the cap back on

Flute: a sophisticated peashooter with a range of up to 500 yards; blown transversely to confuse the enemy

Form: the shape of a composition; the shape of the musician playing the composition; the pieces of paper to be filled out and submitted (in triplicate) in order to get enough money from the Arts Council to play the composition

51

Glissando: a technique adopted by string players for difficult runs

Half steps: pace used by string bassists when carrying their instruments

Harmonic minor: a good music student

   Harmonic major: a less talented music student

Harmony: a cornlike food eaten by people with accents (see above)

Hemiola: a hereditary blood disease caused by chromatics

Isorhythmic motet: when some members of the consort got a different Xerox than the others

Lamentoso: with handkerchiefs

Mean-tone temperament: one's state of mind when everybody is trying to tune at the same time

Meters

Compound meter: a parking place for your car that requires two coins

Duple meter: may take any even number of coins

Meter signature: the name of the officer who writes you a ticket when you put an odd number of coins in a duple meter

Triple meter: only rich people should park by these

Minnesinger: a boy soprano

Modulation: sage advice—as in "nothing is bad in modulation"

Musica ficta: when you lose your place and have to fake the notes

Notes: small folded pieces of paper passed by students during music class

Parallel minor: a music student who is as tall as his instructor

Phase: what teaching music does to your nerves

Piano subito: indicates an opportunity for some obscure orchestra player to become a soloist

Pitch: a tossing motion frequently used by orchestra players to hand in their music

Piu: a descriptive slang term

Pizzicato: a small Italian pie garnished with cheese, anchovies, etc.

Preparatory beat: a threat made to singers, for example, "Sing or else!"

Prima donna: the soprano who generally dies in the last act of an opera of consumption (or, frequently, overconsumption)

Quaver: beginning violinists

Semiquaver: intermediate violinists

Refrain: "Don't do it!"

Resolution: oath frequently made by music teacher, for example, "I'm going to find another job tomorrow!"

Rhythm: a term frequently found in religious songs, for example, "He is rhythm from the dead"

Risoluto: indicates to orchestra that they are stubbornly to maintain their own tempo, no matter what the conductor tries to do

Rubato: German measles

Sensible: this term is occasionally seen in Italian operas, but it is obviously a misprint

Senza sordino: a term used to remind a string player that she forgot to put on her mute a few measures back

Sequence: small, multifaceted ornaments sewn to a performer's costume that sparkle in the lights

Sharp: an adjective used to describe a musician whose opinions are in harmony with your own

Slur: as opposed to madam

Subdominant: chief officer aboard a submarine

Supertonic: Schweppes

   Diatonic: Low-calorie Schweppes

Suspension: the state one may find one's contract in if one repeats too many bad jokes

Tone cluster: a chordal orgy discovered by dropping off to sleep at the keyboard

Transposition: the act of moving the relative pitch of a piece of music that is too low for the basses to a point where it is too high for the sopranos

Trill: the musical equivalent of a seizure

Vibrato: technique used by singers to hide the fact that they are on the wrong pitch

Virtuoso: a musician with very high morals

ROCK AND JAZZ

UP TO THIS POINT, THIS BOOK HAS focused on jokes about European classical music and those who perpetrate it. Of course, most of the world's music is neither European nor classical; and each one of these hundreds, if not thousands, of distinctive musical genres has a history, traditions, and jokes all its own. No one book could hope to do justice to the wealth of tasteless jokes about each and every genre, but this book can at least make an attempt to disparage those forms most common in North America. Some of the following jokes are interchangeable with those about European classical music and musicians; others are quite specific to their individual genres.

◆ What do you call a drummer without a wife or a girlfriend? Homeless.

◆ What do you call a musician who can't afford to play anymore? Married.

◆ How can you tell when a musician has been on the road too long? When he gets up at home in the middle of the night for a glass of milk, he opens his fridge. As the light goes on, he says, "Good evening, ladies and gentlemen."

- What's the first tune a Canadian jazz musician learns? "Take the Train, Eh?"

- Did you hear about the jazz musician who returned his vacuum cleaner? He said he couldn't handle the attachments.

- How many jazz musicians does it take to screw in a light bulb? One to do it; three to get their names on the guest list; and five to ask how he got the gig.

- How does a jazz musician end up with a million dollars? Give him ten million and wait a couple of months.

- Did you hear about the bluesman who was on the road so long that by the time he got back all his songs were public domain?

- How many girl singers does it take to change a light bulb? It doesn't matter; the piano player will wind up doing it anyway.

- This musician dies and goes to hell. The devil is delighted to see him, and comes to the gates to pick him up in a limo. The musician looks in the back seat, and

there's a beautiful new Martin guitar with his name inlaid on the fretboard. "Where are we going?" he asks. "Well, if you don't mind," says the devil, "there's a gig tonight, and I'd like you to sit in." "Fine," the musician says, and a few minutes later they pull up to a sold-out show in a massive stadium packed with cheering fans. The musician takes his place onstage, and as he looks to the front of the stage, he sees that Janis Joplin is the singer. Then he looks over and see that Bob Marley is on rhythm guitar, and Jimi Hendrix is playing lead. He looks behind him and Keith Moon is there on drums! "Wow, what a lineup!" he says to the devil. "Am I really in hell?" "Yup," the devil replies. "OK, band, on the count of three—'Tie a Yellow Ribbon' . . . ."

◆ How many musicians does it take to screw in a light bulb? It doesn't matter as long as everyone gets a turn.

◆ Saint Peter is meeting people at the gates of heaven. A lawyer comes up and Peter asks him what he did on earth. " I was a lawyer," he admits sheepishly, "but I dedicated my life to defending the weak and powerless, and the quest for social justice." So Peter checks his book, smiles, and says, "Come right in, we're delighted you're here! Now just walk down this hall and take the first door to your right."

The next to arrive is a doctor. "What did you do on earth?" Peter inquires. "I was a physician, but let me explain. I wasn't really interested in making money; in fact, I spent my life practicing medicine in Third World countries, and when I retired, I volunteered to work with the poor and disabled." Peter checks his book, smiles and says: "Welcome, we've been expecting you! Please come in—just go down this hall and take the first door to your right."

Finally, a musician walks up. "Welcome," says the saint checking his book. "I see here that you spent your life as a musician." "That's right," confessed the performer, "but I always volunteered my services for benefit dances and charity events; and I spent years giving free music lessons to poor children." "Wonderful," says Saint Peter, "we're so glad that you've arrived! Please do come in—now just walk all the way down to the end of the hall, take the freight elevator down one floor, and come in through the kitchen . . . ."

◆ How many soundmen does it take to change a lightbulb? One, two . . . one, two.

◆ How many stagehands does it take to change a light bulb?

"That's not our job!"

"Five. Do you have a problem with that?"

◆ What's the difference between an A&R man and a snake? The snake has better ears.

◆ How many record producers does it take to screw in a light bulb? Three: two to design the concept and one to actually do it. Or, equally correct: I don't know. What do you think?

◆ Restaurant patron: "Waiter, how late does the band here play?" Waiter: "Oh, usually about a half beat behind the conductor."

◆ These American tourists go on a jungle safari and as they're setting up camp, they hear distant drumming. "What's that?" they ask their native guide. "Drums play, very good; drums stop, very bad," he says. After a few hours, they get used to the drums. The drumming continues for two days and two nights, and every time they ask about it, the guide repeats: "Drums play, very good; drums stop, very bad!" Suddenly, just as they're sitting down to dinner on the third night, the drums fall silent. The tourists are terrified. "What happens now?" they demand. "Oh, no, terrible!" the guide gasps. "After drums stop, bass solo start!"

◆ You can tune a banjo, but how do you tuna fish? By adjusting its scales.

◆ How many bass players does it take to change a light bulb? Only one, but he'll be late.

◆ Why did the chicken cross the road? To show the sax player the way.

◆ How do you get a musician off your doorstep? Pay him for the pizza.

FOLK,
TRADITIONAL,
AND
COUNTRY

- What's the difference between an Uzi submachine gun and an old-time tune? The gun only repeats 40 times.

- What's the difference between an insurance policy and a folk musician? The policy will eventually mature and earn an income.

- What's the professional folk musician's greatest fantasy? A girlfriend with a job.

- What's the best way to tune a bodhran (an Irish frame drum)? With a pen knife.

- How many Balkan dancers/musicians does it take to change a light bulb? 1,2,3 / 1,2,3,4 / 1,2 / 1,2 . . .

- So this Greek singer is brought in as a last-minute replacement while the band is warming up for their big gig. "Look," he says nervously to the drummer, "I'm new, so let's keep it simple tonight. Just give me the beat on 5 and 13."

- If you practice, tune, make a sound check, and sit down to play, it's folk music; otherwise it's bluegrass.

◆ What goes "Jingle, jingle, boom! Jingle, jingle, boom!"? A troupe of Morris dancers in a mine field.

◆ Once upon a time, two beautiful maidens were strolling near their castle when they heard a tiny voice yelling, "Hey, look down here!" They looked down and noticed a small frog on the bank of the moat. "Hi," it said. "I'm really a singer/songwriter, but an evil witch put a spell on me and turned me into a frog. If you kiss me, I'll return to being a singer/songwriter and we can live happily ever after." So the more beautiful of the two maids reached down, picked up the frog, and slipped it into her pocket. "But aren't you going to kiss him?" her friend asked. "You

must be kidding," she answered. "He's worth a lot more as a talking frog!"

◆ What's the definition of a true Irish gentleman? One who can sing "Danny Boy" but won't.

◆ What's the definition of a traditional Irish singer? Someone who sings through his nose what he heard through his ears.

◆ This Irish couple go to their parish priest because they already have six children and feel they can't support any more. "What can we do, Father?" they ask. "Well, being good Catholics," says the priest, "there are only two options you can choose with the church's blessing. You can either abstain from sex altogether, or you can use the rhythm method." "Sure, Father," says the man, "and where are we going to get a ceili band at 4:00 in the morning?"

◆ What do you get when you play a country song backwards? Your dog recovers, your wife returns, and you get your job back.

73

◆ Then what do you get when you play New Age music backwards? New Age music.

◆ What's 30 feet wide and has 8 teeth? The front row at the Grand Old Opry.

Bagpipes deserve a subsection all their own.

◆ What's the difference between an onion and a bagpipe? No one cries when you cut into the bagpipe.

◆ Why do bagpipers always march while they play? They're trying to get away from the noise.

◆ What's another reason bagpipers march while they play? It's harder to hit a moving target.

◆ What's the one good thing about bagpipes? At least they don't smell.

◆ Some scholars believe that the Irish invented the bagpipes as a joke, which they then perpetrated on the Scots—who have yet to get the joke.

◆ How is playing the bagpipes a lot like throwing a javelin blindfolded? You don't have to be very good at either one to get people's attention.

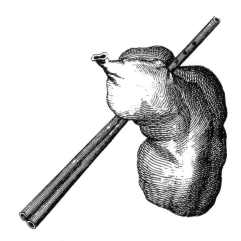

BANJOS STAR IN ANOTHER "bottom-of-the-feeding-chain" joke cycle. In their own inimitable way, they are the violas of the folk, bluegrass, and old-time music scenes. Something should be added in their defense—but I can't think of anything right now.

◆ Banjos are to music what Spam is to food.

◆ Banjos are to music what Etch-a-Sketch is to art.

◆ What's the difference between a banjo and a chain saw? The chain saw has a dynamic range. What's another difference? You can turn the chain saw off.

◆ What's the difference between a banjo and a South American macaw? One's loud, obnoxious, and aggressive, and the other's a bird.

◆ How many banjo players does it take to screw in a light bulb? Five; one to screw it in and four to:

complain that it's electric

lament how much they miss the old one

complain that Earl wouldn't have done it that way

argue about what year it was made

argue about how much it costs

ask what tuning you're using

stand around and watch

Or, alternatively: "None, but hum a few bars and I'll fake it."

◆ How many bass players does it take to screw in a light bulb?

All of them are too laid-back to bother to change it.

Six: one to change it and five to keep the banjo players from hogging the light.

◆ How can you tell the difference between all the banjo tunes? By their titles.

◆ What do you call a good musician at a banjo contest? Lost.

◆ How long does it take to tune a banjo? How long do you have?

◆ Why is a banjo player sort of like an appendix? They can both be big pains; you don't miss them when they're gone; and no one's figured out what they're good for.

◆ Why are all these banjo jokes so darned simple? So bass players can understand them.

◆ Where do banjo players play best? In traffic.

◆ How do you make a banjo player slow down? Put some sheet music in front of him.

◆ What do you say to a banjo player in a three-piece suit? "Will the defendant please rise."

◆ What happens when you throw a banjo and an accordion off the Empire State Building at exactly the same time? Applause.

◆ What do banjos and artillery shells have in common? By the time you hear them, it's too late to run.

- What's the most improbable combination of words in the English language? "The banjo player's Porsche has arrived."

- How can you get a banjo player's eyes to sparkle? Shine a light in his ears.

- Why do so many fishermen own banjos? They make great anchors!

- Why did the Boy Scouts take up the banjo? They make good paddles.

- Why did the banjo player cross the road? It was the chicken's day off.

- Famous banjo quote #1: "That banjo player is no stranger to these parts . . . at least no stranger here than anywhere else."

◆ A touring bluegrass band is convicted of international espionage in a small Third World country, and is condemned to die before a firing squad. When each musician is given a last request, the banjo player shouts: "If I must die for my country, my last request is to play 'Foggy Mountain Breakdown' one more time!" In response, the mandolin player blurts out: "Then my last request is please, shoot me first."

◆ What's the difference between a banjo and a lollipop? When you lick a lollipop, it disappears, but when you play licks on a banjo, it's still there!

◆ Recently, I had to have surgery on my hand, and so I asked the doctor if I would be able to play the banjo afterwards. "Probably not," replied the doctor. "I'm just operating on your hand, I'm not giving you a lobotomy."

◆ What's the fastest way to tune a banjo? Wire cutters.

◆ Which of the following does not belong: herpes, measles, AIDS, banjo players? That's right, measles—you can get rid of measles.

- Why do fiddlers pick on banjo players? Because they can't pick on their fiddles.

- A few years ago a lost group of banjo players was discovered on a remote island in the Pacific. When asked how they survived for so long, they answered, "From the supplies dropped by the helicopters . . . ."

- "There's not much distance between you and a fool, is there?" "Nope, just this banjo."

- Listener: "Can you read music?" Banjo player: "Not enough to hurt my playing."

- A man walked into a bar with his alligator and asked the bartender, "Do you serve banjo players at this establishment?" "Sure do," replied the bartender. "Good," said the man. "Give me a beer, and I'll have a banjo picker for my 'gator."

◆ A Russian, a Cuban, and two American musicians—a guitarist and a banjo player—are sharing a compartment on a train. The Russian, in an attempt to impress the others, says, "In Russia, we have so much vodka that we can afford to throw it away." To make his point, he opens the window and tosses out a bottle of fine Russian vodka. The Cuban, in a spirit of one-upmanship, says, "In Cuba, we have so many fine cigars that they're almost worthless!" He then proceeds to throw a box of the finest Cuban cigars out the window. Not to be outdone, the American guitarist, without saying a word, stands up and throws the banjo player out the window.

◆ Why don't banjo players get any mail? Because they can't read notes.

◆ A banjo player and a guitarist simultaneously fall from the top of a skyscraper. Which one hits the ground first? The guitarist: the banjo will have to stop and re-tune at least once on the way down.

◆ What do banjo players and bottles of beer have in common? They're both empty from the neck up.

◆ The Pope and a banjo player find themselves together before the Pearly Gates. After a little while, Saint Peter shows up to help get them settled. After passing out wings, harps, and halos, Saint Peter offers to show them to their new lodgings. First, they fly to the front lawn of a huge, lavishly appointed estate. "This," Peter announces, "is where the banjo player will be spending eternity. Have a good time!" "Wow," the Pope says to himself. "If he's getting a place like this, I can't wait to see mine!" So Peter and the Pope continue on, but as they proceed, the landscape grows more and more mundane. Finally, they land on a street lined with modest apartment houses, and Peter leads the Pope to a shabby one-room walk-up on the third floor. The Pope is shocked. "Hey, what's going on here?" he demands. "That banjo player got a beautiful estate and I, spiritual leader of eight hundred million Catholics, end up in a dive." "Well," says Saint Peter, "the truth is that this place is crawling with Popes, but that fellow is the first banjo player we've ever had!"

◆ Did you hear about the new Bluegrass Lite? One-third Fewer Notes! Less Picking! Sounds Great!

◆ After you've practiced the banjo long enough, many people will pay you to play; however, your neighbors will pay you to stop.

◆ Saint Peter, wanting the new arrivals to feel at home, promised to spend some quality time with each one. He greeted his first arrival of the day with, "Hi! What's your IQ?" "150," said the woman. "Great," responded Peter. "Let's get together tomorrow to discuss quantum mechanics for a while." He stopped the next arrival and said, "Hi! What's your IQ?" "120," she said. "Fine, fine," said he. "I'd love to take some time with you Wednesday to discuss the current world political situation." The third arrival met with the same treatment: "Hi! What's your IQ?" "45," drawled the man. "Fantastic!" replied Peter. "I've been looking for someone to play banjo duets with!"

◆ A man goes to the brain store to get some brains for dinner. He doesn't see any prices posted so he asks the butcher, "How much are the fiddlers' brains?" "They're $2 an ounce," says the butcher. "And the mandolinists' brains?" "Ah, we're having a special today," says the butcher. "$4 an ounce." "And the guitarists' brains there in the front of the case?" "Those are $5 an ounce." "I'm not sure, they all look good, but what are those all the way in the back?" "Oh, those are banjoists' brains, really choice," says the butcher, "and only $100 an ounce." "$100 an ounce!" says the man. "Ridiculous! Why are they so much more expensive?" "Do you have any idea," explained the butcher, "how many banjo players you need to get one ounce of brains?"

◆ How many strings does a banjo have? Five too many.

◆ What do a banjo player and a human spermatozoan have in common? Both have a million-to-one chance of being a human being.

◆ Banjo players spend half their lives tuning and the other half playing out of tune.

◆ Basic banjo tuning instructions: (1) With a tuning fork: tap the fork on a hard surface; (2) listen to the clear bell-like tone; (3) make sure none of your strings duplicates this tone.

◆ What's the difference between a banjo player and a locksmith? A locksmith gets paid to change keys.

◆ For three years a young banjo player had been taking his brief summer vacations at this country inn. The previous summer he had even managed, finally, to have an affair with the innkeeper's daughter. So, looking forward to an exciting few weeks, he arrived again at the inn, only to find his lover with an infant on her lap! "Helen," he cried, "why didn't you write and let me know? I would have rushed back and married you; the baby would have my name!" "Well," she said, "when my parents found out I was pregnant we had a couple of long talks, and we all decided that it would be better to have a bastard in the family than a banjo player."

◆ Did you hear about the bluegrass police? They're the ones who give banjoists speeding tickets at bluegrass festivals.

◆ What's the easiest way for a banjoist to make money? Threaten to play.

- Another famous banjo quote: "Anyone can play one of them things . . . all you need is three fingers and a plastic head."

- Season and bag limits on banjo players:

  1. Any persons with a valid hunting license may harvest banjo players.

  2. Taking of banjo players with traps or deadfalls is permitted. The use of currency as bait is prohibited.

  3. Killing of banjo players with a vehicle is prohibited. If accidentally struck, remove dead banjo player to the roadside and proceed to the nearest car wash.

  4. It is unlawful to chase, herd, or harvest banjo players from snow machine, hay wagon, helicopter, or aircraft.

  5. It shall be unlawful to shout "JAM," "bluegrass," or "FREE PIZZA" for the purpose of trapping banjo players.

  6. It shall be unlawful to hunt banjo players within 100 meters of Jeep or Ford dealerships.

7. It shall be unlawful to use drugs, women, $100 bills, or PA system sales to attract banjo players.

8. It shall be unlawful to hunt banjo players within 200 meters of acoustic music stores, bluegrass club meetings, parking lot picking sessions, pizza parlors, or Radio Shack stores.

9. If a banjo player is appointed to a government position of senior responsibility, it shall be a felony to hunt, trap, or possess them.

10. Stuffed or mounted banjo players must have a state health department inspection for rabies and hoof-and-mouth disease.

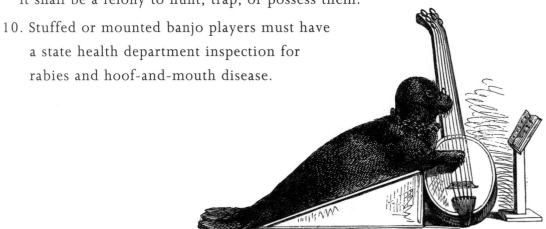

11. It shall be illegal for a hunter to disguise himself as a reporter, drug dealer, female banjo player, pizza delivery person, talent scout, Girl Scout, sheep, illegal provider of copyrighted music, bookie, or tax accountant for the purpose of hunting banjo players.

◆ More famous banjo quotes:

"Frets are like speed bumps on a banjo . . . ."

"Banjos! We don't need no stinkin' banjos!"

"Banjo players never get out of line, just out of tune."

"I bought mine tuned."

"I don't have to take a break . . . it's in my banjo player's contract!"

"Banjo tuning is an oxymoron."

"The only thing worse than telling banjo jokes is laughing at them!"

◆ How many banjo jokes are there? Only three, the rest are true stories.

ACCORDIONS

98

WELL, WHAT CAN I SAY? Probably one of the most frequently disparaged instruments on earth. Belittled by classical, popular, folk, and jazz musicians alike.

◆ Define a true gentleman (or lady). Someone who can play the accordion, and doesn't.

◆ What's the difference between an accordion player and a photograph? The photograph can become fully developed.

◆ Why did the accordion player get fired from the M&M factory? He kept eating all the Ws.

◆ What's the most accurate definition of perfect pitch? The ability to throw an accordion across the room into a toilet without hitting the rim.

◆ This guy is looking through an old junk store down on the waterfront when he notices a gilded stuffed rat mounted on a pedestal sitting on a shelf behind the cash register. He's sort of interested—he could use an odd piece for his den—but he thinks, "No, that's really too weird." Nevertheless, his eyes are inextricably drawn to the piece, so he finally breaks down and asks the storekeeper, "How much for the gilded rat?" "Well," says the man, "it's $100 with the secret, and $25 without the secret." "I can see paying $25," replied the customer, "but $100 is ridiculous! Tell you what, I'll give you the $25—I'm sure I can live without the secret."

So he gives the shop owner $25 and tells him, "Don't bother wrapping it, I only live a couple of blocks from here." He leaves the shop and starts walking, but after a block or two he hears faint scurrying sounds following him. He stops and looks, and there are a dozen rats behind him! A little unnerved, he continues for a few more blocks, but when he looks over his shoulder again, there are hundreds of rats following him! Panicking, he decides he has to get rid of his newly acquired purchase, so he runs out to the end of a nearby pier and hurls the gilded rat into the river. As he does so, thousands of pursuing rats separate on either side of him, and lemminglike, fling themselves into the river and are drowned.

He's thoroughly traumatized, but after a few minutes, he collects himself and rushes back to the junk store. As he opens the door, the store owner smiles knowingly and says: "I know why you're here. You've come back to pay me the extra $75 and learn the secret! Right?" "No," says the man. "Actually, I've come back to buy that gilded accordion behind you."

♦ An accordionist is sitting at a bar nervously fidgeting about himself. "Anything the matter?" the bartender asks. "My keys, my keys" the accordionist replies. "I can't find my keys!"

♦ "Mom," the little boy said seriously, "I've decided that when I grow up I want to be an accordion player." "I'm sorry, dear," his mother replied, "but you'll have to make up your mind. You can't have both—you can either grow up or be an accordionist."

♦ A man walked into this bar and said, "Hey, bartender, have I got a great accordion joke for you!" "See that black belt on the wall, kid?" said the bartender.

"That's mine. I'm an accordionist, and I ain't got much of a sense of humor. See that guy sitting at that table? He's my cousin. He's an accordionist and he ain't got much of a sense of humor. And this here is Bubba." The man looks over at the large, tattooed figure on the next bar stool wearing a black leather Hell's Angels jacket. "Bubba's an accordionist, too, and he doesn't take kindly to criticism. Now, are you sure you want to tell your accordion joke in here?" "Well," said the man, "not if I'm going to have to explain it three times!"

DRUMMERS AND GUITARISTS

ANY OF THESE JOKES ARE INTERCHANGEABLE. Both guitarists and drummers take a lot of abuse from fellow musicians—as well as from discerning music lovers.

◆ What do you call some one who's not terribly musical, but nevertheless likes to hang around with musicians? A drummer.

◆ How can you tell if the stage is level? The drummer drools equally out of both sides of his mouth.

◆ How do you tell if there's a drummer stand-ing outside your door? When he knocks, he speeds up.

◆ How many drummers does it take to eat a rabbit? Three: one to eat it and two to redirect the traffic.

◆ Why do drummers have a half-ounce more brains than horses? So they don't disgrace themselves in the parade.

◆ What do you call a drummer who can't play? An accordionist.

◆ At the bar one night, the drummer came around to all the band members asking for a small contribution toward the funeral of a recently deceased fellow musician. "Can you give me $5 for a colleague?" he asked the bass player. "What kind of musician was he?" the bass player asked. "A fellow drummer," the first replied. "I'd be delighted," the bassist said. "In fact, here's $10—go out and bury another one."

◆ What's the difference between a drummer and a drum machine? You only have to punch in the rhythm once on the drum machine.

◆ At a biology conference, one scientist remarked to another, "You know, at in our lab, we've switched from rats to drummers for most of our experiments?" "Really?" she replied. "Why did you switch?" "Well, for three reason: First, we found that drummers are far more plentiful; second, the lab assistants don't get so attached to them; and third, there are some things even the rats refuse to do. The only problem is that sometimes it's very hard to extrapolate our test results to human beings."

◆ How many drummers does it take to change a light bulb? None: They have machines that do that now.

◆ Did you hear about the drummer who locked his keys in his car? It was terrible; it took him two hours to get the bass player out!

◆ How do you get an electric guitar player to turn down his amp? Put a sheet of music in front of him.

◆ How do you get him to play even more quietly? Put notes on the sheet.

◆ How many lead guitarists does it take to change a lightbulb? One to do it; 99 to stand around and say they could have done it better.

- What do a vacuum cleaner and an electric guitar have in common? When you plug them in, they both suck.

- How do you get two guitarists to play counterpoint? Ask them to sight-read the same chart.

- What's the best thing to play on a guitar? Solitaire.

- How many session guitarists does it take to change a light bulb? Just one, but it will probably require several takes.

- The night before Little Big Horn, General Custer and his troops are camped in the next valley over from the Indians. Just as the general is sitting down for a strategy meeting with his top officers, they

suddenly hear drums. The general turns to his Indian scouts and says, "Boy, I don't like the sound of that; that sounds really bad!" The guides listen closely, nod knowingly to each other, and then reassuringly say: "Don't worry, that's not their regular drummer."

THE WORLD'S OLDEST MUSICAL JOKES

FINALLY, THIS BOOK WOULDN'T BE COMPLETE without the following ancient, moldy, and just plain dumb musical jokes. So, just in case, by some remote chance you've actually never heard these, the author (apologetically) closes with them.

- The oldest musical joke in America: "Hey, mister, how can I get to Carnegie Hall?" "Practice."

- Second oldest musical joke in America: What do you get when you drop a piano down a mineshaft? A-flat minor.

- A man walked into a bar and was amazed to see a foot-high midget playing the piano. He asked about it and the bartender said, "Yeah, well I've got this genie in a bottle who works magic." "You think he'd grant a request for me?" the man asked. "Sure," says the bartender, "but I've got to warn you, he's hard of hearing." So the man rubbed the lamp and asked for a thousand bucks. Nowhere to be found; but when he looked out the front window, there were a thousand ducks! "That's awful," he said. "Yeah," the bartender agreed. "I told you he was

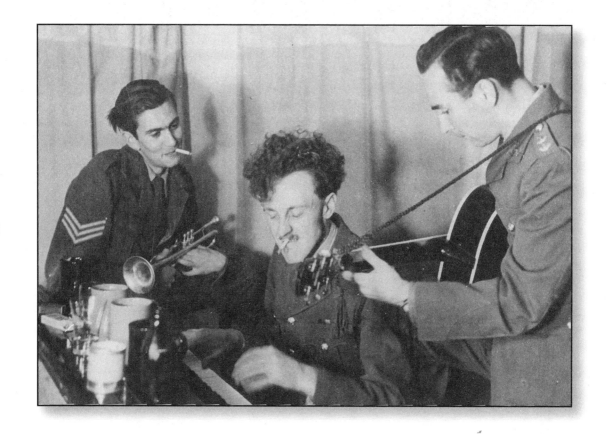

hard of hearing. But now you know how I feel. You don't think that I asked for a twelve-inch pianist, do you?"

♦ "Doctor, doctor, will I be able to play the piano after my operation?" "Yes, of course." "That's funny; I never could before!"

♦ (This one requires two people), First person: What's the most important aspect of telling musician jokes? Second person (interrupting): Timing.

♦ Why did J. S. Bach have so many children? Because he didn't have any stops on his organ.

♦ A musicologist decided to go to Beethoven's grave and dig up the famous composer. When he got to the coffin and opened it, he found Beethoven madly erasing all of his music. "What in the world are you doing?" he asked. "Why," Beethoven replied, "I'm de-composing."

♦ How do you keep a really bad musician in suspense? . . .

Have I missed your favorite musician's joke? If so, please send it to:

N. J. Groce

c/o Schirmer Books

1633 Broadway

New York, NY 10019

I'm sorry, but no compensation or credit can be given, but I'd be delighted to hear from you—and you'll be helping in a good, if tasteless, cause.

Photo Credits

The author would like to thank the following individuals and institutions:

Time Frame/Vintage Photographs/Carole Hedges & Robert Krueger:
  pp. viii, 63, 116

Fred Oster/Vintage Instruments: pp. 7, 23, 37, 72, 97, 108

Collections of the United States Library of Congress: p. 67

California State Library, Sacramento: p. iii